Ruins of Redemption

Poetry in English & Spanish
by
Alvaro Vega

Open Door Publications

Ruins of Redemption
Poetry in English & Spanish
By Alvaro Vega

Copyright © 2016 by Alvaro Vega
ISBN: 978-0-9960985-6-4

Nora H. Añaños,
Translator/Proofreader for poems in Spanish

Published by
Open Door Publications
2113 Stackhouse Dr.
Yardley, PA 19067
www.OpenDoorPublications.com

Dedication

*To my family and friends close and distant,
the Saints and Angels that walk among us, and the
unknown for keeping us vigilant.*

A Note to the Reader

I began writing long ago; it started as just a few lines on paper, a poem here and there, usually very sad. Yet I enjoy that wretched feeling of getting it on paper.

Oh well.

This book was driven by so many things. Growing up in Cuba... suddenly leaving in 1973... not being ready to go... my upbringing in its social, economic, and political quagmire...two staunch Catholic grandmothers...arriving in the States...the old policeman on the bus to the Red Cross office calling me a monkey, a word I remembered almost a year until I translated it in the Spanish to English dictionary. All of these things have influenced me, shaped the way I think and feel about everything in my life.

This book, I hope, tells a story about how I see life and how events have shaped the way in which I embrace it. How, with just a few words, people have influenced me, society's impact, and my family's. Because I am Cuban-born it's impossible not to feel in certain ways about politics or religion.

If I have not interested you by now, don't go past this point. Why get aggravated? Just move on to another book; this one is just sad, please don't read on rainy days.

Thanks to all my friends, enemies, acquaintances, distant family, the crazy and somewhat sane people who have brushed up against me, even if by accident, my parents, my brothers both, my children all, my grandsons whom I adore...and finally my wife.

Every person I know has influenced me. The places I have visited, things I have seen, a glance with a stranger, a word that has inspired or imprisoned me. Please don't assume the poem is about you unless I tell you it is. Sometimes it is coincidence that binds us in this world. Direction in life can have parallels and similarities, either in fortune or despair. Cry and cleanse your soul. I hope it helps you feel better about your own life.

Madness

Your black hair shines with the glow of Europa
Your dress is that of an ice warrior
You lean over and pick up your gloves
And I maintain silence

I see an Angel dressing you
The steel breastplate fits you perfectly
It glimmers and you make it spark with your sword
in a poor effort to make me smile
You're leaving
Will I see you again?
Perhaps next time it will be in a peaceful world
Or in a world surrounded by a single pulsar
I just don't know it's too early to tell
I will miss you; my body will tell me often
My mind will tell me in my sleeplessness
My reality sometimes is altered without warning
In waking dreams of us
Sometimes I know you steal my soul
And bring it to places far away
My only hold to sanity is you
And now you're gone
Gone with no possible logical return

Alvaro Vega

A Sad Day

What am I going to do? When I am no longer useful
When neither my shoulder strength nor influence will help the
Ones I love it will be a very sad day to know
Will they have compassion?
Will they feel sad for me?
Will I be cast aside?
Like an old dog will I die and go back to the earth?
Will I be remembered?
Will I still be loved?
Will they feel sad for me?
Who will kiss my face?
And say a kind word
To be useless will be a sad day to know

Presidio

Here inside these castle walls I find an unbearable boredom
Not far from these walls you can find my friends and
Comrades in games, hunting, laughing and sharing life
You can find my emissary
out there, my foe he hunts for me
So I must be here
He will never cease to look for me; he is cunning and able
His strength is not of this world
I know
I have confronted him in battle
I am acquainted with his blade
Death
I have been so very close to it
I still remember the smell
He will someday meet his hunger for me
The inevitable will come to pass

Alvaro Vega

The Hand of God

Same as the Phoenix my heart rose
From the amber and dust to meet the love that you
So kindly place upon me.
And the Angel smiled and then laughed
She asked why I was so sad
I said I love you more than life itself
Then I saw the same tears of a million colors taken
By the wind, same as I saw in that mountain this winter
She said it's easy to forget that I belong in heaven
That you are much greater than what I will ever be
My beauty and strength is heavenly and that I can't help
My stay here ends now and I am joyful that you are safe now
My mission is a success

I am pleased that I was chosen to walk some time with you
Joy that through me the Universe sees
I bow to you and thank you
You share the brotherhood of humanity and you are kings
When placed at our side
I said
Will I see you again?
Yes
At life's end so you have no fear

A Storm Is Coming

Life has not been easy today
It squeezed me hurtfully hard yesterday
Broken and disconnected I move through the spider web
To my credit I am moving
I will not stand still
Fully knowing the imperative
I know that I will find Atlantis, it's not far now

The tightness of the death embrace,
 the sound of bones breaking
The hard gasp for air, the tears and questions of why
I fall today far and deep
I am not desperate but I am not at peace
I am accepting of what is coming
I have taken it—I will be brave
My turn will come
I will take the form of a hurricane
On an unexpected season
Paint myself with fury and hate
The colors of war
Life is good now you say
Good and God will prevail
Like He always does in my life
Everyone is saying be calm, be cool

Alvaro Vega

Three Stars

Three stars ignored by time and great distance
Hang in the northeast sky
Like diamonds or demons always in December
As I gaze the heavens
For something lost that I can't explain or point to
I gaze with the wonder of a child forcing my eyes to get closer
As I gather light of a billion years
and pour it into the deepest recesses of my eyes
And command them to bring me there
My fingers play with the light and I bend it up and down
on this cloudless dark night
and as I look true north the faint smoke of your fire
brings me closer to you
you hunt the wolf and keep us safe, I hear his howls
your cape, hard and weathered, has held out children
lovingly many times, magically soft when near a fire
I close my eyes and I see your boots
gauche on the Earth and ground cover

Leaving behind the mark of iron and hammer
and your steady confidence
to complete the hunt
Your heart lives here along with your soul
as your spirit soars far above us all
we share it, we will never cage it—it is free
like the falcon that roams this mountain
that screams whenever you are gone.

Human Us

Oh mighty Lord, how is it that
I find myself here at your feet?
Tell me?
Your hand has been my guide,
my sword free to bring pain and death
To those who will not yield to your will.
How is it that I find myself here at your feet?
Is it that I am weak?
Is it that I can no longer be your angel of death?
Or is it that I am becoming human?

I Beg for Time

Every word I know I run through my rusty mind
Can't find the true expression for this moment
So only tears will I offer

On my knees my hands open to heaven
Much more I can't give
I am lost in despair and deep sadness
Please don't look upon me
Oh mighty God. don't look to me
Your gaze will hurt
Time, I beg for time
I beg for death
I beg for life
I beg for mercy
Only tears will I offer

Alvaro Vega

El Español Bizco

El amigo de él odia a la criada,
la criada odia a la Señora María.
María odia a don José, y el joven Carlos odia a María
Ese odio profundo que se surge sin querer.
Y al final todos odian al español Francisco,
que anda medio bizco y odia a todo mestizo,
ya que él es "Castellano"
Y nadie más, que no pertenezca a su casta,
es digno de entrar a su casa.

The Cross-Eyed Spaniard

His friend hates the maid
the maid hates Mrs. Maria.
Maria hates Don Jose and young Carlos hates Maria.
That hate is strong when it is found suddenly
and at day's end everyone hates the Spaniard, Francisco

Who looks at you crossed-eyed and is a racist, as he hates
everyone. He is "Castellano"
And none of it can be shared in conversation
Because if not of the same tribe don't dare enter
his home.

All This Crying

Thanks for asking. I did cry today
For all of those vistas that we were part of
I cried for all of those smiles that my eyes caressed in you
Your coquette gazes that made me want you so
My desire in seeing you made my heart warm with love
I cried all of those distant times that
I so much want to return to
I cried all the rainy days we spent on the coast of Greece
I cried your white dress
I cried your silk skin
I cried the day you lost yourself and
I showed you the way to me
I cried the day you found me
I cried the trust and passion that you had for me
Now you're not here and I cry
In the distance I see that Peace can be acquired and I ask
Almighty God to bring it to you
And I ask only mercy for myself

What From Here?

I ask Gods any and all to forge my heart in a bath of steel
and make it as strong as a second century spear
and then you say something so beautiful
my heart sings
What am I going to do with this diamond, you?
Sweet, sweet woman what awaits me?
I am dusty, broken; am old, I have an enormous ache
that swims in a sea of uncertainty; and discontent
Drowning me slowly in the most peculiar way

Alvaro Vega

The Condor's Flight

At sunset I kneel here, my eyes overlooking centuries past
Gazing at these ruins under my feet
the ones that hang on the side of this mountain
My tears flow and fall upon this land
I pray and weep for the tormented ones,
for the ones that felt the whip of the Master
that live to suffer in a set task to survive
my eyes burn
It's the cold wind of the mountain
What of the condor? Riding the thermos of the canyon walls
The souls of the long departed
command me to be strong, consuming precious living time
they also weep and plead to me to move on
to look at history and learned lessons.
I conclude my prayers as a Cardinal stands
and asks all to be seated
Pope Saint Francis awakes to thoughts of today,
the Eucharist front and center
The heaviness and hounding thoughts of children hungry
Pressed by the urgency of humanity's thirst for Christ
Average Joe reading books of fantasy, some academia,
detective stories
Today I think of bringing bread to my mother
hoping the sky stays up,
Well knowing in advance how perfect my days are planned
and how insignificant it all is
made not the world better today, no Sir

Always Loved

I saw you adding flowers to your hair today
I stopped and admired in silence
You saw me and smiled

Your face has a radiant beauty
You leave me breathless every time I look at you
Your dress flows over your body like silk in the wind
I want you with all my heart
Don't ever leave
Stay here with me forever
Always on a throne
Always on my mind
Always loved.

Suppression of Reality

With hearts of lions we take the hill,
my eyes burn and I miss clarity
It could be dirt or dust or simply suppression of reality.
Some of us fall in this hell that we have surely created;
I sense fever and fear, can't seem to get all the flies
and bugs off my wounds.
As we reach this sad summit my eyes clear and I find
myself
looking over a valley of palms,
 then the stretch to the edge of
beautiful emerald green waters with gentle surf.
I see how this is as close as I will ever get to such paradise
hell is between us

Alvaro Vega

The Dark Room

In the dark room he sits tied down without rope
He can't get up
He certainly has legs
From time to time in the darkness light reflects on a face
Sometimes a face that is angry
All these faces have voices
Stern voices
Soothing voices
Screaming voices
Castigating voices
Voices without any remedy to silence
This will send terror through his very being
Some of these voices make him smile while others
Give him outstanding advice
But he is always paralyzed without ability to get out
A prisoner of himself
Many times knowing that the room has no windows or doors
The unparalleled terror of knowing he is in a box
A box where he can feel his breath
A place where his throat can speak
but will never let him scream
In part he cries to God in a beggar's voice
Why me? What have I done? Have I shamed you, God?
What is wrong with me?
The surroundings of his world is a painful silence
Without real voice, people move behind glass
Only the cold wind passes and caresses his beautiful face
His body asks for rest unknowingly,
with very little significance
His voices are the only things that have any importance
He knows it is evil to hear and pay attention
But to pay complete attention is a matter of life and death

Bring Time In

I come from Enceladeus to see the carousel of infinite time
as it flicks on the flexible metal teeth of reality
and the owl sends the carnival music in,
all happy tones that serpentine around the red and brown
leaves of Autumn on Earth

I know that the Gypsy girl will run to meet her family
on the promenade,
she knows that time changes everything,
everywhere, without permission or parade
She is perfectly at peace with that rule
because her life has just begun
The tells of the old woman's cards and dried bones
promised her that only good fortune awaits.

Always With Me

These days whenever I am galloping in my mind
through the plains of Mongolia usually in the mornings
then later following the flight of an Angel far into the
mountains of Coconda, Angola
or simply completely detaching and going for a walk on the
warm sands of an island
You're always in my sky, in the air I breathe,
on every carbon fiber
deep inside my metallic, robotic heart
just before I arrive at true reality
that is my hellish life
these days

15

I Feel Pain

With great disdain I will ignore it
I will shake it off because I can

My world shatters
No relief and I will ignore
My frontal mind begs for peace
And I ignore
I raise my arm, the palm of my hand open
I will ignore
I will set up the traps for the wolf and his companion
Sustaining the pain because I can
The moon will be absent soon
And darkness will fall upon the face of earth here
Darkness with its steel teeth and suffocating reach
Sustaining pain because it can
If you can't you will be sad
If you can't you will be dead
If you can't you're erased
If you can't the world moves away.

El Mensajero

Son las diez y media de la noche y todo termina. Todo termina
aquí en el nublado anochecer.
Y es en la sombra de la oscura noche, cuando el El mensajero
cubierto con el polvo de su larga travesía, bajo su oscura capa y
Sus botas llenas de fango, con el dolor de sus ojos secos.
Exhaustos de tan pesado y largo viaje, con dolor
en su corazón por convivir eternos
días, tal grave mensaje.
Al fin el largo viaje termina, sin embargo, no habrá fiesta, ni
sonrisas, abrazos.
Su recibimiento solamente traerá angustias lágrimas y
enfados, y al fin seguramente, quizás ni agua se le ofrecerá.
No por falta de cortesía, sino por falta de conocimiento y razón.
Se pierde el equilibrio cuando tal noticia llega,
se pierde el hablar…
Y hasta el correr de la sangre, se hace difícil, a causa de tan fatal
noticia.

The Messenger

It's ten thirty; it's all finished, at this time it all ends.
The messenger with his long dark,
dusty cape and muddy boots
And painful dried eyes, bows his head ending his journey
With heavy conscience and carrying a note with bad news
It all ends now
There will be no joy nor smiles nor hugs
Only tears, anguish and anger
In closing his task, water will not be offered to him
No fault at not having courtesy
but more at not realizing his persona
Equilibrium is lost even speech

Blood rushes to the head
Time completely stops
The messenger leaves.

An Accident

As I cross the forest line
My boot finds a stone and I fly head over heels for seconds
I land on gravel and blue grass long stems and luscious green
I have an arrow in my heart
My quiver is full; I haven't pulled on my bow in some time now
I sit up and think, probably days ago
The last time I was near that ridge way over there in what is
my inept horizon
How could I have been so careless?
A seasoned traveler
The entrance wound has become crystal black
Can't be concerned now there is no time
but once I get to the Athenian falls
I will pull it out myself
Those damned ghouls!
I will ignore it all now and enjoy nothing
Just sip on the nectar of rage
Those damned ghouls!
This has never happened to me
They run into me annoyingly sometimes
And go their way,
they bow those horrid heads as a subspecies should
With respect and humility always very timidly
Why are they hunting me now?

Lost

The other day I paid attention
to how sand fell between my toes
my feet bright as bleached wood
in solitude, in the most inconsequential moment
In my right hand I held a crucifix
that a Saint blessed long ago
plain and simple as God may have wanted it to be
its power of good surrounded me
my body, I realized, in part belongs to this world
to its rules and discomforts, to its critics and
well informed, those that steal my time
As I in other ways continue an endless struggle with
a capricious desire to be right with the heavens
to see past the limits that have been imposed on me
the uncomfortable need to question
all the implications of a single moment in time.

I See Me

Dreams of titans and songs
The Vatican is always at hand
I never fall on my sword others around me do
Always in the name of honor
The scenes change rapidly and traces
of nothingness are left behind
I hear the Pope whisper as if summoning someone
I always know it's not me
In the obligatory dream enchantment
I see men at war, I see fire and swords
I see hope and confusion, courage, coward man
I see me.

Alvaro Vega

Gather All the Angels

And bring Mother Teresa,
have them show me the way to heaven
A mountain climb from here, despicable, I am distressed,
disarmed, dishonored with anger.
Then, only then, go and gather the Saints
the new and the old world ones, the good ones
and the not so good
have then all the Archangels drag their swords
on and above me on the gutter
as I look up
my tears will surely dry on the way down my burned face
as I beg God
to please kill me where I stand
today I see nothing, faith eludes me
my heart is an empty vessel

Can't you see? My soul has left me
I grasp and claw at the deep waters of my misery
I crush memories and lessons inside my mind with vigor
I feel no love, no clemency at conclusion.
To my chagrin I see no hope
That's the moment that faith begins to elude me
I have in remorsefulness walked the nights looking at the sky
in the same way I have looked at it in daylight most of my life
to never see a sign, never a message, "the ruler" of the sky
Where are you, God?

Eres

Veo que eres pobre,
veo que le pides a Dios,
veo que súplicas por gozar de otra vida,
una vida mejor, llena de riquezas.
Yo te regalo la mía,
incluso mi entera y total fortuna,
mi reloj preferido,
mi casa del campo,
mi casa en la playa,
el apartamento en la ciudad, donde nunca duerme
mi tristeza y dolor causados
por la muerte de mi mejor amigo,
mi perro leal y fiel,
el peso que deja cada año Viejo,
la nostalgia por la familia lejana,
todo el oro que tengo y el dinero que resta,
el amor de mis hijos,
el adiós de mi madre,
una inesperada despedida,
la muerte de mi abuela,
te regalo mi coche nuevo,
todos los días de sufrimiento y
mis noches de desvelo.
Te dejo mis pequeñas y grandes preocupaciones,
te dejo mi fama,
mis amigos y enemigos,
mi pasaporte, también mi ropa,
mis anteojos y zapatos,
mi sueños y anhelos,
mi música, mis canciones, mi bandera, mi conciencia,
mi avioncito de juguete que tengo en el buró de mi oficina,
una pluma y un bello escrito,
el dolor de tres cirugías,

la memoria de un hermoso atardecer,
la memoria de una cautivadora sonrisa…
peticiones concedidas, ya no eres más pobre,
ya tienes una vida mejor, llena de riquezas,
ya ves?

And Then There Was Light

You are not comporting correctly in God's birthplace
He sees you killing without reservation
He sees you day and night planning evil
With your heart full of hate
He sees how you poison the innocent
And how you oppress the poor and feeble minded.
He sees how the violence circles
From camp to camp, among you the minority the genius
At times the majority asks for peace, to no avail
And round and round you go
And he increasingly becomes less and less patient and
tolerant
If you only knew how he holds in his spirit the great fire
and the lightning, the cleanser of souls
He will let you see in time
He knows in your time of infinite madness
you will cry to an open universe
He is sad and angry. Can't you see?
You are human. You hold no other power in his eyes
your name is written in the book of life
Have compassion to one another or
Be stopped, be erased.
"In the beginning all was without form and void
and darkness was upon the face of the deep"

Remember Me

Remember me
On a rainy day
When I lost my horizon
On a cold day
When my bones hurt
On a fall day
When the leaves fell at my feet
and the flowers left me
Remember me
On a beautiful day
When you have no worries
On a day that there is nothing on your mind
Remember me
On a day that you touch that ring I gave you
on a day when the memories of me caress your soul

Remember me
on a moment of rest
Remember me
one day when I am no longer here.

The House of God

The house of God is with me.
This house is everywhere I go
I am sure of it.
Do you see it?
I have seen sickness and injury, and he's been there for me
I know how it all has made me stronger
In a cold world
With habitant snakes.

Claire's Light

I swing the axe at the mounting ice
Trying to get some weight of my vessel
It's November now and Superior will sing
The gales will embrace me in a dance of death
My soul will shake when my body calls for sleep
I am poor disposed out here

Below these icy waves I sense tranquility
Succoring me today, the Patron Saint of Cuba
Way out here just for me
My mind betrays me, clarity begins to feel cold
I am brave, a simple man, my home this vessel, its name
"Clara luz" a play on words "Clear Light" or "Claire's Light"
with a Nor' West destination
as I signed the book at Saint Marie's
Now desperate to find Thunder Bay
I will let the gale lead and the Saint guide me
And someday I will pour some of my
white label Scotch whisky
at the broken blue ice that grips with fury the shoreline
under the clear light of the moon.

No Justice

Holding on to apathy
Pushing your way through life
No compromise
No prisoners, everyone is executed
No regrets
No skeletons in the closet
No memories
No laments
No confections
No forgiveness
No justice
Holding only to violence
Running amuck
Ending your life
Nothing in your mind
Empty mind
El fin.

My Cape

I see my demise
I see an end
I see it on the walls of this cave
I place my hand on a stone and a fast growing root of ice
ascends my fingers
I feel more like a marble carving down here
—my sweet earth
I no longer hear the beat of my heart
Death is my cape
I move around pensive and it swings away and back
I see my demise I see a beginning.

25

Alvaro Vega

Deity

Maria, Mother of God
Protect me in the world of today
strange and complicated
With so few similarities to the past
Maria, Mother of God
Highest and most important Saint
I don't know how to pray to you
I don't know the protocol
I know nothing it seems, only how to beg
Maria, Mother of God
Save me
Give me a secure direction
I am lost
Your Son looks away
I have no destination I am without a Road
Maria, Mother of God
I have no one

Save me

María Madre de Dios

Protégeme en el Mundo de hoy,
tan extraño y complicado,
nada similar al pasado vivido.
María Madre de Dios,
Altísima y Santa eres, la más
ponderosa.
No se cómo orarte, desconozco tus
plegarias.
Parezco no saber nada, pero sí se
suplicar.
María Madre de Dios, sálvame,
dame dirección segura…
perdido estoy.

Tu hijo no me ve
Sin destino, sin camino seguro,
no tengo a nadie, ni tengo a donde ir,
sálvame.

The Night Wind

I don't dream about vineyards anymore
"la Campagna" as it's called—I found it in flames today
I stood on the road with axe at hand
The ambers flew in the night wind
The moon large and vigilant
same as in Toledo that summer of ninety-four
the shadows of vines and grapes smirked with cynicism
and they danced to the sound of cracking timber
not much I could do, but to admire the strength of the fire
in the distance I heard the bells—can they be the church bells?
I am not sure; why would the church care?
Cascade of memories would follow
and tears would fall all around me on that dusty road
I looked down could not bear keeping my eyes fixed there
my hands they look broken and dirty
My boots old and weathered
Am becoming part of this place, this land
The mountain to my north the town below this hill
The flames are now higher and I fear for the sky
My mind feels numb,
there is no place closer to heaven than here
The crystal clear waters of the Mediterranean sing to me
The Saints answer my prayers, the Angels protect me at will
I have found contentment and everyone loves me
Now "La Campagna" is gone a museum piece lost to inferno
Should I stay another season?

Yo Amo a Dios

Por el verde sendero paseas de mano con tu querido,
y con la otra acaricias la cruz de tu cadena.
Tu cadena, la que te hace rezar,
la que te hace mentir,
la que te hace juzgar,
la que te hace superior,
la que no te da angustia,
la que te hace feliz,
la que te hace olvidar,
y entonces la cruz,
la que te perdona,
la que acaricias al morir.

I Love God

You walk the promenade holding hands with your lover
The other hand caressing the cross on your chain
Your chain that makes you pray
That makes you lie
That makes you judge
That makes you superior
The one that gives you no grief
The one that makes you happy
The one that makes you forget
Then the cross
The one that forgives you
The one you will caress at death

Fortunate

The fortunate son – I never was
as I leave Montenegro due South on the waters of the Adriatic
I tie my bloody sword and armor and I heave it overboard
I curse the universe—I will embrace death before war again
Marching toward you for years; can't seem to reach you
a vagabond, mercenary, a pirate—not liked by God
today away from the fire of the battlefield
from the soup of horror, screams of death and desolation
The angel Gabriel punished Satan, it was horrific

My eyes now burn with sadness for men loyal who are gone
I keep a tunic that is no longer white like the snow of home
My heart has no red because time and tears have washed it away
My hands are cold and have forgotten the soft touch
My eyes will betray the presence of beauty
Love is now committed to memory because
my soul will not let me forget
I am steady as I tack South East
And find the trade winds of the Mediterranean
I love you; I love you—I keep whispering like a madman
I know it for a long time now
I have been blind, by darkness that old witch
now setting a course to a place leagues behind me
pulling away, forced by the lamenting winds
I stretch my arms to the horizon and I see Poseidon
Menacing me as always
I will, I will
find my way to you, I will.

Alvaro Vega

My Worth

A red sunset and for the first time in many years
I look in your eyes
I see every smile you gave the world
I see the world as you see it
I see that not all your seasons were mild
I can see every animal you saved
The kindness in your touch
A red sunset and I look into your eyes
And see the world as you see it
I also see how weathered my hands have become
I realize how much more you could have had
your choice was me
I am a shell
My worth a few coins, that's all, no more
You look into my eyes
You smile

Enola

Enola every time my eyes see you
my soul pains
You and your belly ended a great war
Saved countless lives
every time I see you
my eyes fill with tears
I hurt for the heat of the Sun that your belly created
I cry today for the ghosts of all wars.

Night

The campaign has been on now five years
My mind is pit gravel numb from the hell of war
My uniform has become comfortable now
I instinctually do things that keep me alive
My eyes are always dry and when I think of the past
I always want to return there, then I realize
That it all has vanished like the smoke of my campfire
I know that someone on a sunny day will find me
And I will shed the endless protective plates
that keep me alive
Including the one over my heart
I will leave this note here on the ground where I rest tonight
Same as I have done almost every night
The acid rain and fires will destroy the paper
Long before anything alive walks this place
The earth will take them and keep them,
lost words, silent words
The words of a soulless mind, hopelessly lost without a home.

Alvaro Vega

My Flag

Badly injured he wants to protect his flag
Now overtaken by the enemy he doesn't care
will not turn it over to anyone
He unmounts it from the pole he has carried now
A million days with very little rest
The blades cut into his soul
And he begins to fold it
The blades cut into his life
A lightning flash of his mother
Congratulating him on his
Fifth grade graduation and promotion
He folds again and again
And the blades cut into the canyons of his mind

When he is finished
He stands in silence
And he places the flag inside his overcoat
And buttons it up to his bloody neck
only an empty pistol now
He draws his sword, raising it up high to the sky
Showing God and the Angels
Then he falls
He falls on his back, mortally wounded
Looking at the blue and bright sky

Cuándo fue que Llegaste?

Ciego en esta neblina, sin cielo y tierra,
sin espíritu, rendido ante tanta Soledad,
sin café, piel húmeda y solo un fósforo, aquí en mi ayer
rozo con mis uñas sucias un pedazo del presente,
aquel que se quedó aquí a mi lado.

When Was It That You Got Here?

I am blind in this fog without sky or earth
Where is my spirit? Giving it all to Soledad
No coffee and humid skin, only one match
Here I sit in my yesterday
Reaching with dirty nails for a piece of the present
As it comfortably sits at my side.

A Gift to You – If You Want It?

I'll give to you my life
My fortune all and complete
My favorite watch
The house in the country
The hut by the beach
The apartment in the city where I can never sleep
The pain of the death of a good friend
My loyal and loving dog
The weight of every year I get older
The missing of faraway family
All the gold I have and all the money that remains
The love of my children
The death of my mother
A hard goodbye
The death of Grandma
I give to you my new auto
All the days I felt pain
The sleepless nights
I leave you my worries small and monumental
I leave you my fame
My friends and enemies
My passport
My clothes
My glasses and my shoes
My dreams and necessities
My music, my poems
My songs, my flag, my conscience
My tiny toy plane I keep in my office
A pen that writes beautifully
The pain of three hospital stays
The memory of a lovely sunset

The memory of a bright smile
I give you every warm hug
There is more I'll give you
Time to decide.

Are You Free?

To be truly free
Free to walk along all the trails on every mountain,
To walk the plains, and deserts on Earth
To be truly free
Be free to love, live, sing
The fantasies of a captive mind
A heart in a quagmire of barbed wire and high fences
Never a guard and yet
A complete and permanent detention
To be truly free
Where is my Heroine? Where is she?
With a wire cutter and a long black cape
Black boots, black dress, red lips, and a soft touch
To be truly free to change destiny
The fantasies of a captive mind.

Alvaro Vega

You

You wake up summoned by a mission and you hear gunfire
You know that sound well and it's very distant now
You're neither upset nor surprised,
as you walk across the room
Your eyes are on me, I smile and you look away
Your beauty is stunning
You try to manage your hair and give up
As your index finger hunts a cigarette out of the box
you light a match
You inhale
Your eyes close
You steady yourself
Every second now I see a flash, a photo in time
a painting in canvas in my mind
As the colors begin to bleed into this reality
you appear as a magical dream
You look at me without a sound
I feel your gaze on my bones then my life
You see everything I am
I feel cold, and then I see the fire of your eyes
My world shatters
You put the cigarette out mechanically and begin to move
seconds before your fingers move away from the ashtray
You blink once slowly and your lips kiss my face
I close my eyes and you kiss me again
I feel you so close to me now
and I can't bear to have you move away
You hold my face in your hands and you kiss my lips
I know that soon this moment will end
I know that my heart will desire this moment always
I know I will forever be in love
and eternally lost in your world.

El Sillón

El sillón de mi vieja,
fuerte y bonito,
cuando había cigarro y café
Calma y risa en un verano eterno,
A veces sin calma y sin risa,
en el mismo verano eterno,
Y hoy la quisiera aquí
sin juzgarla, como
extraño tu sonrrisa

The Rocking Chair

the old woman rocking in her chair
strong and beautiful
as she had cigarettes and coffee
calm and smiling in an eternal summer
sometimes without the smiles or the calm
or the cigarettes or coffee
in the same eternal summer
and today I want her here
to simply say, "te quiero Abuela"
I miss your smile.

37

Alvaro Vega

Fear

I fear the Nor' Easters of Huron
My compass is always set to Columbus
South to Ohio
thinking of the pub you and I had a drink of scotch
Before the storm
The winds of November
always cause my eyes to tear up
Your banishing never helps
when the rains come
My face has taken on the weather
and now it has less of an affliction to expression
A card game is always welcome here in my solitude
If only the moon would leave

The mean sea level,
the mean low water
wouldn't confine me to my vessel.

Chained to Home

I now fear going to Saturn.
Old souls can be lost way out there
This fear is real and pressing
The horror of being gone from reality
with no hope of sweet return
This makes a stronger barrier
That will always keep me close at home.

Así o Asa!

De una manera o otra, he sido amado
ciento sesenta otoños.
No siempre debidamente
pero amor es amor y nunca
se desprecia, amor es amor.

So and So

One way or another I have been loved
One hundred and sixty autumns
Not always proper but
Love is love
Should not be dismissed
Love is love.

Ask God

Through the sandstorms we travel blindly
Please guide us
I see a determined direction
I don't see an off-ramp
A change
A contemplation of distance and arrival
I see a runaway marathon without a place to call an end
I ask God
Please help us
He will not answer
We keep to the task

Alvaro Vega

Day Under the Southern Sun

Pelican walks the shoreline
an honest and true man limps
and a friend extends a hand
as the manta ray blows the sand away
over and over on the shallows
of this calm lagoon
a decent woman in a black hat chats with an ancient man
he swims like a fish and sometimes argues with his shadow
Two women, one telling jokes and stories as the other laughs

A Jewish man rinsing a garment, then a swim
As if by magic three men go under, aqualungs
a terracotta paradise and the sky gives nothing away
a titan falls and bullishly gets up with
new ideas and promise to survive
with no pain in the mind but much in the heart
lights on the water, then darkness as you move
through the night
a chef and more from Russia to India and around the world
with the spider at his shoulder,
something that only a few will ever see
a fallen vampire is remembered
with love and the family grows
orange is looked at with newfound respect and purpose
and the southern Sun sets as the condor takes flight.

Twelve of Us Here

On this island
We dress in soft cloth
Set out to the shore
So we can look out to the Sea
We like terra firma
But we love the Sea and the Sun
We play in the Sea under its blue canopy
Fish its waters, too
Two times now it wasn't tranquil
Two times now we were afraid
Someone from the green house
Was taken by the Storm

We think into the Sea
There are twelve of us here now
If you lick your lips you will taste salt
It always smells like the Ocean here
No one will leave
We want to stay no matter what
How sinister the Sea becomes
We will cover our eyes in the storm
And be afraid
We will go to the shore and look out to the Sea.

Alvaro Vega

Every Moment

We paddle this rickety canoe along the banks
of this river, the foliage is adequate
the old dog meets us at the shore and he brings the sun.
The truck sits cold, not sure it will ever run again,
I will never leave this place
You sit by the water
I wade in
I feel in my heart every moment we ever had,
I look back to you saying my name, my heart awakens
The reflecting rays of the sun crown you
and the Angel Gabriel danced with joy
You verified my existence with every smile every gesture
I lived every moment, as if an eternal dream
lived it in the splendor of your love
and sweet protection.

Memory Rattles Inside My Mind

As it begins it is only a widget
Then color begins to take its rightful place
It all begins to appear as if by magic
Then more silence
As it all bounces inside the mind
Sounds of Mother in the Kitchen
More color then coffee
I then have a middle
I never panic about an end
It comes on its own
Usually with much noise
I lean in and tone it down

Day in the Sands

White sugar sand and a warm summer
Light breeze with a taste of salt on the lips
my gaze to you as you step over the side of the skiff
Quick, pull yourself to shore
your hand over your eyes
you scan the horizon looking for me
with the cunning of an osprey
so in love, you find me and smile
You now look away and I wonder

What tells will you have?
What love tells of centuries past will you share with me?
Will the heroine melt in the arms of her lover?
or will she cast aside his love?
my heart beats faster and my breathing becomes shallow
I will kiss your lips soon, the salt will not matter
Only you and the sweet of the cherries you hold in your hands
will consume my dreams and capricious desires tomorrow.

Alvaro Vega

At 50 Yards

As the war coach, an old green scud missile launcher begins to
move, serving me as transport, I motion my cousin
the driver to stop.
I step on to the sidewalk and there at 50 yards stands the
hero of this old, dusty and dirty revolution
Once a proven soldier with unquestionable resolve to
command, now an old man
I stand at attention as my mind races to find a voice from far
away in my youth that yells
the correct way to stand at attention, as he sees this he gently
moves his wife to his side, inquisitive of my action
I raise my right arm and extend a military
salute to this old man
I see how he musters all his will and strength to steady himself
and returns it equal to me at 50 yards
I relax standing at attention. I turn and step
back on the transport
As it begins to move again I look out the window and see him
holding his wife as if taken with emotion
The moment I turned away was the last time my eyes would
ever see him
No matter how misguided one is, one can always find
humanity even in hearts of iron
A symbolic gesture could make fire cold
It could make the iron shield stealth
It could make an uneasy soul relax
What it will not do is ever ease tyranny

Footnote: *I hold a few memories that I will take to my grave with
great sadness. The one of me saluting my uncle that April of
1994 as I was departing Havana will stay in my soul forever.*

Dime

Dime cómo es que con amor me mientes,
enséñame por favor
quizás algún día yo encuentre a alguien,
que quiera como soy,
que quiera como es.
que me miras a los ojos y me dices que me amas
y ya tan temprano me traicionas,
cómo es, enséñame cómo
último acto de amor
enséñame
enséñame
te lo pido como último acto de piedad.

Tell Me

tell me
how is it that with all that love you lie
show me how please
maybe someday I'll find someone that loves like I love
how is it?
that you look in my eyes and you tell me you love me
and so early on you betray me.

Alvaro Vega

Mind Fever

We walked under the tarp and you got to see a circus
No one stopped us—you asked about the clowns
I disliked them long ago they came from Russia
Drunken I am not, wish I was
God oh God here is my hand

Where are you?
Now I am in a place flat and full of sand
to the four points of my compass
I turn and turn in place—is it this way?
yesterday Africa called for me
I wanted to go, I didn't
Then today Lima, the mountains
Why?
God oh God here is my hand
Where are you?
My head spins
The fire in my mind returns
Everyone pleads for me to be calm
I can't—why?
God oh God here is my hand
Where are you?

I, Procyon

I daydream in class every day
My dreams carry me to fantastic places
Setting out always alone
I always get a smile on my face, it's a dead giveaway
Harshly and abruptly I return most times
With the welcome slap of a wooden ruler hitting my hands
The pain? It's sinister, rude, cruel and indecent
It hurts too much and it cut into my heart. I tear, yes
My eyes always betray me with deep lakes of tears

I never make a sound
Tilting my head back slowly so no one sees me
To keep my tears inside my eyes—it never works
The beautiful girl that I so much admired from far away
Now looks away
My body is here, my thoughts go to places I send them
—yes I will always do that
No one controls my mind I am free inside here
Free to fly away so far that neither lies nor pain catch me
Who created this place? Why all the cruelness?
I wipe my tears away
I am dreaming again this time of a Palace
and a beautiful princess
Here now I am a knight on a black horse,
It's spring and there, there
Can you see the butterflies and rainbows? She smiles I am free
Oh that smile that gives me away returns.

Alvaro Vega

El Tesoro del Pirata

Al pirata de Somalia,
le gusta tirarse al mar,
buscando tesoro o algo para brillar.
Su escopeta está oxidada,
y es por eso que el cojo no le ofrece nada,
Y rema y rema por su Tesoro,
buscando agua profunda
Agua de tomar, con su escopeta sin valor,
se ríe el pirata de Somalia, y se marcha sin encontar nada

The Somalia Pirate

Likes to go out to sea
Looking for treasure or something to eat with a rusted gun
is why the gimp will not offer him a thing
And he oars and oars to deeper waters
Looking for his treasure
The pirate that looks for deep water
Water to drink with his worthless rusty gun
Smiles at the pirate of Somalia and finds nothing.

Heaven's Shield

The dream of running naked in the Andes
Tantani's clouds disappear in my low horizon
now I slowly walk through the snowy incline
My legs warm like when I played as a child in Habana
Smiling as the wind serpentines around my body
I raise my arms to the clear sky
I can't see past the blue shield of heaven
God wouldn't let me
I look away from the wind

It doesn't feel easy to walk here
Waiting for something to happen
An explosion, a sound or something, anything
There is nothing here that I can see
Where are my clothes?
What is that in the distance?
It's dark and red and it flaps to the west
Same as the wind
Moving forward and backward
Why here? I wonder
What does it want of me?
the dream is getting away from me
awake, awake just leave the footprints.

Alvaro Vega

Icy Mountain

The Gypsy woman feels the fire in her blood
She slowly walks to the window;
the old song comes back to her
as the man runs his fingers through his jet black hair
picking up a fedora, then runs out
to jump in a taxi, ride to Cape Cod
The Gypsy woman stays here
because she feels fine and spins and spins
Silence in her mind and ears
as the music plays loud outside on the street
the paperboy leans on a post to see the spectacle
He smiles the moment she winks at him, he shyly looks away
she turns into the hard turn that requires her talent
remembering dreams all made of fantasy unique and complex

warmth and caring everlasting, comforting
And the whales sing past the Ice Mountains and short
Peninsulas here on the windy icy coast
the music runs like the wind bringing autumn
The tempo begins to fall and sadness appears in the music
Tears also make an entrance, she lets the moment be
in her slow spin she brings the castabelles above her head
Tears fall backwards from the exotic pose
of her abandoned heart
She steps hard into the next note, her eyes wet
as the fire in her soul dries the pain
and delivers her into the night.

E Voi?

I cross the grand patio of the Cathedral
onto the granite slabs that suddenly front the café,
she stands promptly
and assertively says "Posso solo amarti un Migliaio di anni"
previsto!
e voi?
I am speechless and the world becomes silent,
slowly I begin to hear the church bells again
and it is she that says, "Che e piacevole, il mio amore?"
My eyes swell with tears and I am overwhelmed
she has given much more time than I deserve
she is stunningly beautiful, her eyes are true
she considered and decided
I will not fail her
I embrace her
I am overtaken by the warmth of her love

Alvaro Vega

I Just Can't

The sharp strumming melody of an acoustic guitar
along with African drums will
Always boil my blood and bring me back to childhood
The fever is too great to contain
A million pictures of hot dusty planes flood my mind
Black beautiful faces—Carola y su hermana
The history of us
I look at the sky and cry for answers
They will never come
I will always refuse silence over outrage
I will always prefer war over injustice
It can't be nothing more anything less
I just can't
Am I crazy, God?
Why is it that iron chains of Earth
Are not enough to bind me?
No answers for me?
Up to me then?
With minimal attention
Minimal guidance or direction
Expected to die in a cave
Or create miracles
I just can't
How grand life, how easy to just be alive
How sad it makes me sometimes

Prison

The lightning flash that is life
Makes my eyes swell with tears now
Not long ago I would set sail out of the Bering Sea
South to the Mariana Islands were the Sea is deep and giving
The cradle of my world, my life
I now sit and wait for my end
as everyone reminds me of my yesterdays
Time is finally a friend, the one that holds my hand
Where did all my men go?
Did they sail away and leave me here?
In my mind they sail forever
Ageless like the clouds and my beautiful Northern Star
strong and vigorous, determined and bright
Always looking to overtake the prison that time gives light
I now reside in my colorless and eternal here
And I wait and wait.

Red Lines Hurt

With tears falling and slitting down my face,
I lift my hands toward the fury of the fire.
My hands ask for the pain to stop
this human crime right now
my eyes fall to one side and I see humanity
crying in great despair.
I feel the heat embrace my face
and like warm water something falls at my feet,
a raging river of fire runs down my chest
and the red lines hurt my skin.
I stay as I am
I find myself soon in the distance
as the eagle moves on.

Alvaro Vega

At the Heights

At the heights of the Wheatley's I saw all my demons dance,
Dance in gory lust and me and a friend shield them
from the truth
She loves me and I her
Not the cheap love of a walk in Milan or
the passing fancy of silly lovers on a fall afternoon
as the entire world judges
an honest and clean love untainted that hurts no one

Goodbye

Intoxicated by a medley of love
Sent here by the Gods
I embrace the passion that it inspires in me
On my knees one shoulder to the earth including my face
In this rain forest of illusions, reality lost purposely
I clearly see you so far away
In your high boots walking that ironclad rotunda
dressed in black, no armor
You smell the essence of my life way out there
I see tears on your angelic face
My eyes are captured by a raindrop that slides
on the aged glass

The droplet slows and stops
My eyelashes scrape on the wet earth
Rescue me not, come to me and guide me to the stars
my heart beckons your warm breath close to my face
this last Sunday one final time
as my broken body desperately tries to come back
in a futile effort that makes the Saints weep.

La Entrada

La copa puesta encima de la mesa con urgencia,
ya que se ve el vino derramado.
Media botella queda y allí, las ventanas dejan
entrar en aquel Abril, el dulce
aire de la mañana, las cortinas suavemente
se deslizan a un lado,
el sol resplandeciente hace su gran entrada,
aquella alfombra que la vieja nos obsequió,
aquel perro sato que duerme en la tranquilidad,
qué lindo silencio de aquella mañana.
El tiempo aquí no corre como en otros lugares.
Aquí es diferente no hay urgencia,
no se tiene que hacer hoy ni mañana,
aquí este momento es ya y después,
aquí llegan los cansados y los que van de prisa, aquí
vienen todos los que llegan temprano,
Y los que llegan tarde y se quedan
un tiempo y nunca pueden cantar
Todos intoxicados y la única expresión es una sonrisa.

Alvaro Vega

The Entrance

A chalice placed on the table with urgency, the wine stains it
Half a bottle is left
the windows are open and that April
the sweet air moves aside the curtains.
The sun makes its great entrance
on the carpet that the old women gave us, the dog
sleeps in tranquility
Beautiful silence that morning
Time doesn't run here the same as in other places
here it is different
there is no urgency
No need to do it today or tomorrow
this is the moment of now and later
arriving tired and pressed for time
and everyone who is on time
who gets there early
the late arrivals, they stay for a time
no one can sing
Everyone is intoxicated
the only expression is a smile.

Roses

A night for the roses a night full of stars
in the background a dark blue sky
With the aroma that conquers in the midst of its shadows
Open to the infinite night sky
The rusty gates of the garden swivel in a light wind
And the night belongs to the roses.

The Saint

Shielded from the flames of a burning world
You guided me and showed me a heading that got me
fortune
I see that now
You guided my hand at difficult times

"Acaena liberare, cingulus"
I am focused, I am sharp, and I am centered
I miss you now, Maestro
Thank you for helping me in completing my journey
you were here the perfect amount of time
Rest in peace Maestro! My friend!

Alvaro Vega

Beckon My Stealthy Swim

With the slow passage of time in this lagoon
I often feel the day's heat will surely kill me one day.
But it all changes in the evening as if life
embraces me all at once
and the Ocean calls for me again,
the deep cold currents beckon
my stealthy swim
the change of the ocean's currents will be pleasing
I always know that others follow
I can sense it.
But it's all the same to me
I am one here, it all belongs to me.
On my return the day begins all new
and I receive the sun and all its splendor,
then find myself back in the morning
warm again.

The Blue Sun

Your eyes are my bridge to Alnitak
They bring me there with ease
You are my key,
my key to the infinite wonders of the universe
Your gaze sends thundering waves
that distort the state of matter

It pulls on my flesh and
the tranquility of me
I hold to the edge of now
and you hold strongly to me.

La Aurora

Baila, baila Aurora, que poco tiempo te queda
Te deslizas en el horizonte
Ni permiso,
Ni súplicas,
Ni disculpas,
De lejos te hacen bailar
Y todos te miran
Y a tí no te importa,
Ya acostumbrada estás
Y qué?

Ya la claridad se acerca,
y con odio te retiras.
Sin adiós, ni flautas
Sin teatro, ni cortesía.
y dejas atrás la máscara del anochecer.

Alvaro Vega

Maybe Someday

It gets real green out here in summer
But then again it's green all year long
I sit and look at old photographs of winter days faraway
So many loved ones gone! So many
I hold a photo in my hand and the reflection
of my old face comes back to me
from the wavy glass of that wet window
I think and think—why am I alive?
I place the photo face down on that table
where so many have shared time and laughter with me
they are gone now forever
My life has been too long, too hard, and now at its finality

I get to see all my loved ones depart from my world
Is this the punishment of vampires
that don't get the wooden stake?
I am numb, sadness has finally inured me
The payback of a time thief
Stolen time that finds me an earthly hell at end
I pray daily that my return to this world
will be shorter next time
To this time-locked world, with unforgiving life rules
That have punishingly shaken me
Maybe someday someone will be sad that I am gone
Although I suspect that they will be happy,
I have lived too long
Maybe someday.

*To my dad and his brothers ("the vampires"); my grandfather on
his last night on earth said to me, "ya ni se cuantos anos tengo,
estoy cansado" I can't even remember how old I am, I am tired—
he was 103. Sometimes death is sweet to those who have lived.*

Beginning

Your skin has taken the beautiful tone of this place,
mocha and a light red tint
Just like the earth around here.
The flat ground rises far into the sky at its crest
A flat surface to the stars
Night comes and my soul flies far away
My arms touch all the southwest stars
I will be affixed to this place soon,
My start, my center point, my end.
You gaze into the universe,
not so far away shine Venus and Jupiter
Your hand points to a faraway galaxy
Your touch makes it ripple away and near,
then it sets back to its perfect place
I turn slowly and you are gone
A golden feather bright as the Sun falls to the red earth
I place my hand under it
Lightning cuts across my body and mind
I wake up alone on a bright and beautiful day:
The seventh day of the seventh month
In the year of our Lord nineteen hundred and sixty
Strong and full of life.

Alvaro Vega

Fray and Fire

I sat down through a long and sad eulogy
Nice words were said about me
and also the dead man there in the front
his feet pointing the door out
I was surprised and embarrassed
Finding myself reflecting on shallow rain days
And disappointing times
I will not be reaching heaven like the preacher said
this man would
the dead man, with the steady walk
he will
I am certain
As he was a good man
Away from the fray and fire of hell
Safe and comforted by soft light and a good woman
Smoking cigars on Sunday over the land and wood rails
Warm sunbath in the early mornings
with a good hardcover book

Never going there near hell because it wasn't required
Above the heat and lava of the color red
And now at death a speedy ascend to the heaven guard
with understandable ease that he would enter
Godspeed dead man
find your place in the stars

Bring Death In

I run four hours and sleep two. I have all my gear
This is a vast place very little for me to consume
Locusts would never survive
There is a great need to stay sharp
The destroyers of worlds can only follow at night
I can now say after a few days on the run
That I am ready to bring the fight to them

I hold a Saint Christopher's medal and an old cross
The Pope's open hand touches my shoulder,
he wished me well
I hear all the Saints crying
Looking at the dark and cloudy sky
I see the Angel Raguel running the blade "sobre la lija"
And sparks of fire fall upon the Earth
Doomed I am—no one has to say it
I will walk and fight till life leaves me
At some point my spear will fall and my body will not
Michael said
Do not underestimate the power of a strong conviction

Alvaro Vega

Sueño elegante

Quiero enseñarte mujer un camino en el mar,
donde nadie ha ido,
donde el viento de primavera acaricie tu piel.
Donde tú serás el único ser de tan lindo lugar.

Donde el fuego de pasión y amor no lo podrás detener.
Donde siempre caliente estarás.
Donde tus manos se estrachan a mí con delicado pedir.
Donde al fin completa te sentirás.

Elegant Dream

I want to show you, my love, a trail in the sea
Where no one has been
Where the winds of spring will caress your face
Where you will be the only beauty
Where you will not be able to detain the flames of love
Where warm will always be
Where your hands will reach to me in a sweet plea
Where at end you will completely be

Your Revolution

I received news of the revolution yesterday
I read it slowly, stopping at some passages I smiled
Not sure if because I saw untruth or if I saw indoctrination
I thought of you and your archaic direction and confusing life
Also I thought of the Saints, remember? The ones in our youth
The Saints, choose death to satisfy
and ratify pure direction never compromising
You're not a Saint but your heart is free, true, and pure
Yesterday's news was in color,
and very sympathetic to you and your cause
I was lost in your words my proximity to you was felt
I should argue the context of your words
but I just don't have that fight in me anymore
the reality is that I miss you and all the insanity, still today
am lost presently trying to understand your position
your cause the one that tears you naked and makes you feel
like a true revolutionary, alive—what does it do to me?
It rips the skin away from my body adding salt on the pull
I will hold the words in my hand for a few moments perhaps
I will walk on the hills and let my mind wonder

Alvaro Vega

Corona Obitus

Corona Obitus, a child whispers
Every angel is here
Their wings so brightly white, just like Luke had said
Full open and standing on sacred ground
I look at my feet, the road is gone
No longer is it now
I see all my yesterdays fighting here
Then
The colors of the solar winds howl like hunted wolves
My bloody hand firmly holds a crucifix
The angels look to the heavens
Then
They're gone
I reflect at the beauty of fire at end
Alone.

My Name

You walked over to me this morning
and found me alone in the dark
I am Loneliness—have we met?
Did I see you around here before?
Could have been the time you overnighted in Reno?
The long stares at the Long Island Sound this past winter
Bench warming near the fields of the Oakdale Arboretum
Perhaps it was the walks on the white beaches of Key West
It had to be you; you had the same look about you.
No worries; everyone is welcome here
No ticket necessary, just take a moment, a day, or years
The sun will not be, and never touch these windows
Bring your heart it will just be me and you.

Linda Casa de Campo (Campaña)

Ahí entre esas dos lomas cae el río, y en esa loma a la derecha
se levanta todas las mañanas, esa humilde casa de campo
con sus palmas a la espalda.
Y su finca y espinas a su puerta
Raices que huracán nunca a movido,
con la bendición de Dios,
Aquí casi nunca se pasa un segundo.
Pero a veces con amor uno se fija en tan grande belleza.

Beautiful Country House

Over there between those two hills falls the river
and on that other hill on the right
I built that beautiful Campagna, a simple country home
In the background palm trees
Every morning this simple and loving home
lights up with the morning sun
With its sugar canes, lemon trees and thorns at its door
Roots that no storm ever has moved
With the blessing of God
A place of joy a home full of love
And sometimes everyone stops
to gaze at the beauty of the hills.

Disillusioned

Standing with a long lance at hand as
the mountain wind plays with your flag
At the beginning of a very long walk
here your eyes can only have a short and small horizon
The tall pines know that it's fall and send
their intoxicating fragrance
mixed in with the morning air
The green scent hides the smell of steel
You're a tortured soul without conscience
A general without an army
I am sad for you and your quest
But I will not tell you
Pity is lost in minds that have become blind
I will only follow at a distance
The truth is that you will never notice me out in the wind
and only your flag will matter.

The Getaway

I want to run now and go as far as my legs can take me
All I have to do is get away from this choking hold
This place
find a trail, any trail will do
My legs will not fail me, my spirit will drive me
I will create distance between me and this place called
Boredom.

Drink From This Fountain

I found this fountain by accident on a walkabout
Alone and old, older than most
Not shiny but intricate
I come here every day and sit
Sometimes all day now
All I have now are my memories and the Sun
I know that sometimes I fall sleep
Because I wake to the yells of young children
"Sveglati Vecchhio"
I have been here too long
I don't go to see the blue arc anymore
It gets too cold for me now
If I had someone to love me
Perhaps they would be looking for me
I must go home
to who? and why?
Maybe I will stay here tonight
I would love to see my stars again
One last time
Through my hazy eyes
Then, then, then…
"L'uomo vecchio e morto"

Ezio

Ezio, tall at the helm
Smokes as a defiant act to weather
Waves break over the stern
Ezio blinks to clear the salt off his eyes
Steady, tall at the helm
Points toward land at starboard and laughs at adventures past
The storm screams and we get concerned
Yet steady, tall Ezio is at the helm.

We keep to our stand
As the sea judges and administers punishment
It doesn't matter if only time is exchanged for distance
And as much as we lament our now
We know Ezio will get us home.

The Fall

Yesterday just off that ledge I leaned and very slowly
My hand gently reached for the face of an angel,
her eyes were closed.
Her skin was softer than any silk found in the east.
Her eyes opened
and I fell for a thousand years
Then she found me, she did
and that afternoon
I found myself safe at home.

Las Rosas

Una noche para las rosas, noche con estrellas,
la aroma que conquista entre las siluetas negras
Así abiertas al gran esplendor nocturno,
Las rejas oxidadas se mueven en la oscuridad,
en el suave viento de la noche y esta noche es de las rosas.

Lend Me a Hand

There is nothing here to love everyone is gone or missing
This existence is so relentless it drones on and on
There is no way out of here; it's a maze
I finally concede to loneliness
Can't go through any of these dead-end walls
Every second I grow more and more desperate
Will I ever find my way?
I am looking for that hand to be extended.
I reach and reach and I get nothing only find a tempest of
darkness and emptiness.

Alvaro Vega

Her Life

She takes the drink and kills the pain
Drinks by day only
all the others, the sinners, drink by night

When it becomes late it's only because the night rushed in
When she can't recall the day before, she looks at her age
When it becomes clear that new friends need be found
It's only because everyone has moved or died
The pain comes and goes and her life slowly goes
She thinks and thinks and sees no farther
Her day is long and sometimes too short
She will rush at a moment then sit for an hour
Her life goes, her friends go,
She finds her way, she goes away,
and she is loved and happy today.

En Cualquier Noche

Los vámpiros se deslizan por los callejones en el crepúsculo
Las señoras con confianza celebran su juventud y la noche se pone
más cerca
Y el peligro se pinta de rojo,
Y camina casi sonriente,
Y las conchas marinas cantan,
Y alguien arrastra algo,
Alguien se detiene,
La llama de una cerilla enciende el Tabaco e ilumina la noche.

Whatever Night

The vampires slither into the back roads at twilight
The ladies with confidence celebrate their youth and the
night gets closer
And danger paints itself red
And walks about smiling
And the seashells sing
And someone drags something
Someone stops
The flame of a match lights the Tabaco and illuminates the
evening.

Alvaro Vega

Here Are My Words

So the words start flying with some thought
Unstoppable, better to have been held in.
What is said now stays
 like paint that begins to stain a tarp, for all to see
the indignity

How dreadful the slow warm burn of blood rushing to the face
Soon the cold follows.
Is this moment soon to end?
The here and the now is eternal
And someone smiles, and another laughs
a feeling of belonging comes again
The body relaxes and soon a smile appears
all is well again.

Hoy

My spirit flies close to that comet, the one near
the swooping eagle
It's summer on Earth and I am in a triangle
Hunger, despair, loneliness
I shouldn't come out this far anymore
Its never good for me
Nor for the treasures in my kingdom
I will lose myself out here someday
And no one will miss me
No one misses me now

I have tried to return now for nearly three light years
Time flies around here.

I Call Your Name Out Loud

Knowing that you'll never answer
The places are usually desolate damp and cloudy
As I look down, the ground is always muddy
I wear boots, my battle boots
I again yell your name to no one there
Only me, and what is a place on Earth, way away

The log rolls as I pull my legs closer to the fire
The flying amber snaps as it finds the night air
I bite into food that I found in my bag
As the rain begins to fall
I see gray and dark green colors
The air is cold now, winter is coming
I have forgotten how to rest
So I repair my gear
the rain runs down the leather straps
as if looking to find an opening, a new road
it falls to the muddy ground
Am I the same as the rain?
Will I find that new road?
Or will I fall to the muddy ground?

Alvaro Vega

I Walked In

I came in up ten incredibly unsecured floors
made a turn at the window near your soul
You wonder how?
your eyes let me; they betrayed you and trusted me
I walked through a museum frozen in place
kisses with warm hugs in glass boxes
Found hanging labeled pieces
of care and love from many years back,
broken empty stands that held souls that are now long gone
I would stay as long as am wanted in this lonely heart
To make it whole again, to make it live again,
to make it sing and dance again
To skip on the cape of night in winter
on some sidewalk not far from here
To push away ruins that have become treacherous
To do away with fences that serve no purpose
I will build on long forgotten fields that no one visits now
I will plant security in your beautiful land

I will raise your flag at the heights, point and salute it
because I hope you will become my Queen someday
I will love you eternally.

In My Mind

In my mind the world is perfect,
no doubt, no pain.
Inside my mind all is in order
It's always in order in times of chaos
I smile and all is fine.
In my mind there is never any pain
it can't get in unless I let it,
sometimes I do by accident, sometimes I am careless
wish I could hold the pain of the complete universe
 inside of me forever
and never let it leave…
I may be able to stand it
I am almost sure, I think, maybe
If I fail in such an endeavor
Then I will be sad, not tranquil.
and if I am destroyed?
What of me then?

Stardust with essence of you
All memories that I keep of you
Gone, finished.
Why? Why universe? Why?
Why so cold?

Alvaro Vega

No

Don't ask me just for fun
Don't pull me into your madness and crazy dreams
I will not be amused to
"walk through the valley of the shadow of death"
I am pretty sure it's not safe there
I will not cross a major highway on foot

No, I will not pet that barking dog; he foams with hunger
I will not ask that arguing couple for the time
I will not yell immigration anywhere
I will not travel to a third world country
without a passport or visa
I will not yell anti-communist slogans in Habana
What did you say about swimming with sharks? That's a no
I will need a compass before
we parachute into those mountains
As for getting on a train as a hobo
I am sorry, I am going to have to decline that also

Are you seeing how worn out I am?
No? No wolf hunting this year—I still can see the bite marks
Where did I find you?
You say that you have always been here
How is that?
Friend, please let me be now
This vessel is finished. I have lost all my love for adventure
I have lost all strength.
Here, take my crucifix; take it on into your madness.

Juzgadoras Arenas

Mañana consigo un equipo de paz,
y vamos a gaza con la mona de la ganadera
si no tenemos suerte,
nos perderemos en los vientos de octubre en el Sinaí
y la arena nos juzgará

Tomorrow I will get a peace team
And we will go to Gaza with the beauty that lives on the farm
If we do not find Luck
We will lose ourselves in the winds of October on the Sinai
And the sands will judge us.

The Valley

In a valley of granite and stone
The sun tries in vain to discolor the ground
I stand and my boots are hot, it doesn't matter
I stand on the ruins of our home world
It could be any name on the old maps
No one knows
This is more than I could have imagined
This is greater than me
To begin again
How do I find the strength?
Who will guide me through the fog?

Alvaro Vega

My Lord

The bells of Saint Francis resonate this cold winter morning
they made you cry a day long ago
you look up as if summing up that day once again
The bells grace you today like that day in September
As you walk up to the steps
you see the enormous front window
With all the Angels
The Angels make eye contact and bow their heads

you feel at peace and safe
Out of the stone marble the arms of the Saints, delicate
like porcelain Lenox with a milk glass polished shine
and absolutely holy reach out to you
You bow your head, your heart runs back
to the beginning of time
The old wooden door is open
and you step into the house of God
Your eyes find Jesus way over there
On an eternal cross, forgiving you
Sadness touches your heart
Your right hand to the holy water
You curtsy in view to all including the Mother
You whisper a few things in Latin
The Universe gives you entrance
You pray hard to Jesus, with humility including the Saints
The Cardinal speaks of faith and the love of mankind
You remember all the good souls that have departed
Tears fall upon you; your skin senses the warmth

Kneeling now your mind on fire and concentrating
a complex process of prayer

pleads for God's grace
You pray for the welfare of others, for mercy
and a general look over to you
If not too much trouble
Jesus speaks to you with signs always
Something falls by Mary and gets your attention
Two snow doves fly across all the Stations of the Cross
Illuminated by the painted windows
blues, yellows, reds, and brilliant white
They land on Saint Lazarus who stands by his dogs
As a loyal Shepherd would, he's by your side
Michael's foot on Satan's throat, the sound of chains
You have God's complete attention
The rosary gleams and the count begins
You cry and pray
Your eyes close your mind moves among the holy
your heart is pure

Your sentiment true
Your soul soars
a beacon of light.

Alvaro Vega

Lágrimas

Te diré que hoy lloré
Lloré por tí y nosotros
por todas aquellas vistas que compartimos
por sonrisas que mis ojos acariciaron en tí.
Tus miradas coquetas que tanto desee.
Hoy mi impaciencia por verte, me hizo sentir escalofríos,
en el centro de mi corazón. Y lloré.
Lloré por todos aquellos tiempos distantes,
que tanto quisiera que volvieran.
Lloré aquellos días fríos de lluvia en las costas de Grecia,
Lloré tu vestido blanco,
tu piel de seda.

Lloré el día que te perdiste en tí,
Y yo te enseñé el camino hacia mí
Lloré el día que me encontraste,
Lloré tu pasión y confianza en mí.
Ya hoy no estás y lloré.
En la distancia veo que la paz aunque lejos esté,
un día colmará mi vida, le pido eso solo a Dios por tí,
y que tenga misericordia en mí.

Pinks and Nails

Pink, mauve, red
What do you say
When it is only colors
There is nothing more
Enter colors of beauty
Colors of love

Now it's right
She likes them all
She likes the attention
Love is what she wants
Kindness comes easy
To those who want it
Cool mornings
Early mornings
Pink, mauve, red
Colors of beauty
Colors of love

Alvaro Vega

Lluvia

Ayer llovió y todo frío y mojado,
el techo de zinc de la casa,
cantaba una linda melodía.
La vieja hacía el almuerzo y con lágrimas suavemente,
le murmuraba algo a su madre:
El ángel que nos protege a todos aquí.
Sentí lágrimas rodando hasta mi brazo y mi mirada volvió a la
lluvia.
Y allí cerca de mi madre quise haberme quedado por toda la
eternidad.

Rain

It rained all day yesterday, everything cold and wet
The metal roof was singing a beautiful melody

Mother made lunch and I saw tears in her eyes
She whispered something at her long-gone mom
The angel that protects all of us here
I felt tears fall on my arm and my gaze return to the rain
And there close to Mother I wanted to stay a complete
eternity.

Man in Armor

She is at command
She covers her steel black eyes from the blue Sun
She is calm on this summit
Sounds of war below
Sounds of war close in
No one speaks
With cold calmness she moves among the granite-cut men
No one looks at her here
Her voice is law to proceed
She is an Angel by God's word
She is the destroyer of tyrannical man
No one cries here
We march into madness
She directs us to where we need to be
We feed because she is cunning
We are victorious because of her strength

We miss no one because she is mother to all
We will return someday when decided only by her
We are the granite-cut men
We march into madness.

Alvaro Vega

Misery and Religion

It is the soup of fire
Seeing from here that some live with short arms
Extending them with eagerness to reach the golden rings
When in fact at end it's always determined
That the price was eternal peace
Give me wings God I am so close, more so than yesterday
I can't be any faster
Give me wings God
I, in principle, want to dismiss misery with ignorance
Then the space behind my eyes a traitor to me
screams injustice
I shout silence, silence, silence.
I am held tightly by religion: my God,
my church, my heart, my mind
Now I am mixed up in a war
Pray, and have faith, time heals and God will provide
How can I pray? I am not so favored
I find a silent God
I am dismissed always screaming
My prayers go silent in flight
Because I am me

My Shoes, My Hands

I was about twelve then
Sitting on a bench behind the iron curtain
I was at a church. I know it because the bench was warm
I, as every child, was looking down at my shoes
Shiny, well made for Russian
Black and very small nice shoes
Sitting on my hands, I pulled on my right one
From under me, it was so small I thought
I looked up for no reason and I saw a man standing
I will someday be that tall
and my hands will be large and strong
I will be far away from here
and my shoes will be large and black

Today in a moment of sadness and despair
Not thinking much about that rusty curtain
Far away from that church on a very cold bench
Listening to my heart beat
I looked down as I sit on my hands
Alas my shoes are now bigger
And my hands?
as I pull them closer to my eyes,
wrinkled and tired

Alvaro Vega

La Prima de España

Con preguntas sin respuestas, una luchadora mujer
en exilio, vive diaria desilusión.
Las cejas arrugadas y un buen libro en la mano,
Quisiera matar al Español de Valencia, quien
se burla de ella al llevar la prescripción,
simplemente porque no sabía,
cómo "pomo" se decía en correcto Español.
Ella expresa "ese idiota Español"

Cousin in Spain

The everyday exasperation of a woman in exile
With some dissolution
her brow tight and wrinkled and a good book under her arm
She then kills the Spaniard Casanova of Valencia
Simply because with her prescription at hand
She kindly asks for her medicine in not the correct manner
All this drama because she says the word
"bottle" using a synonym without the proper tone.
idiotic Spaniard, now he is dead, no do-overs.

Her Struggle

She climbs out and away from this dirty, dusty place
Her cloth all turned colorless, she reaches for her hair
She grabs the tight curls and pulls them back, dust falls from them
Falling to an uneven and unsteady ground
She sighs as if already done with morning,
but she knows it only begins here
her struggle

Water, she thinks it takes over her mind,
a precious need, a great desire
the want of cake—a waste of time!
Her youth all but gone now
She picks up her cargo
Walking and stepping down into her journey
the birds take flight
The mountain shadows at her back and the sun begins to rise
On her east flank the ocean gleams
she has a good pace now and her mind goes to a place of rest
and numbness
all that matters now is this endless walk
nothing more.

Alvaro Vega

To Write, to Speak

Can't write today the pain is too great
Can't see the words, they go past me
Can't recognize what they mean
I know the words, I have seen them before
I try to grasp them and I can't
Everyone thinks I am weird because I don't speak
My language has stopped
I should be able to speak, to command the words to dance for me
They should comport themselves proper
Oh, to write, to speak
What now?

Nuestro Elian

Yes come with us
We will save you
We will give you, life
We will give you love
Yes we will know your needs
We will care for you
We will adore you
We will also guide you
We will know what is good for you
We will reshape your thoughts
And heart
We will show you water and
Explain its danger
We will profit from you
You belong to us; we will give you fame
And hold you here
We are artist's musician's actors
Activist's teachers
We are intelligent clergyman
We are always right
God is always on our side
The only morality is the one we know
The only path is the one we show you
Forget paternity here we are
Mother dead
Her soul now free, all that matters
Our will is law we have the freedom so let it be so
We can hold anyone in contempt

Alvaro Vega

Our Queen

A garment sewn with insults, adorned with injustice
a lovely scarf, knitted tightly
with choler and a cape of discontent
Given to a dame that digs her heels
in a ground of sadness and betrayal
She looks for that exit that will give her fame
or a reprieve from this world
of old colors, deprived of the perfumes that she once loved
Today like Cleopatra she adapts to survive
and compromises always to exist
and the cobra hisses and slithers away
like gears in the catapult worn by time
and splintered by the use of war
She will stay and endure and be called our "Queen"

Photograph

I carved a figurine of you
From a strong dried piece of wood I found in the desert
I took two nights to finish and now
I tightly hold in my hands
I keep it near me
With my broken spirit
My decaying body
My shattered mind
I hold it tightly in my hands
Without my ancient strength
It is what I can keep in my now
What may well be
The last that I see
I am grateful

The Captain

The Captain arrives at six thirty as always
Looks at me and looks away as he says
The men are well rested! Have they eaten?
I know he isn't looking for an answer
He can clearly see, as he pulls the canvas back
The men lined as far as the eyes can see
As he turns I see the frown on his face
He unsheathes his sword and begins

I will send thousands to death tonight
As he wipes the blade on his shirt
I want the hardest one hundred in the front with me
I say—as you wish!
Have any news of my grandson?
I say no
He grabs his helmet, hardened steel, scratched, and dented
Two slits so his eyes can scan the death fields
So his soul can count the fallen men
So his heart can pray as it cries
I bring his horse and realize
we are both so far from home
we battle again, I will clean the chair
where he bathes on his return, there next to the river
the blood will run the waters of the Bay once again.

Alvaro Vega

Por allá y por acá

Cementerio a un lado de la escuela
Y nadie lo ve
Comienzo y final
Hoy y mañana,
y nadie lo ve
Escuela a un lado del cementerio
Y a nadie le importa.

Over Here and Then Over There

Cemetery next to the school
And no one sees it
Beginning and end
Today and tomorrow
And no one sees it
School next to the cemetery
And none care

Setting a Rod

I found God in a Village up North not far from here
He was sitting on an old stump as I walked up to him
He looked me over and said that my hair
and my nails were too long
And that I should wear a hat in the Sun
Also that a week from Wednesday
 it was going to rain hard for three days
I was appreciative and said thank you
I didn't have any questions for him
I just looked at him as he set his fishing rod
Just like my brother loves to set his
He was meticulous in setting it
he held three different size lead weights in his hand
before deciding on one, the hook was shiny and simple
he was done now and he gathered all his things
we said goodbye, walked a few paces and stopped
he then said, "Nothing more from you?"
I thanked him for all the lives around me that love me
Yes I found God in a Village up North
I trimmed my nails that day
had someone cut my hair short
God was going fishing and I was going with him

Alvaro Vega

The Gift

And the hand extends across time and place
it looks to give a great gift to someone special.
And the hand is blocked at every turn,
and we all know who is blocking that saintly hand
we look the other way and now we are marked
branded in our souls
Don't hide it show it—you're branded like me
everyone can see it—they can see in our hearts
Why hide it?

The Old Women's Song

Calm waters is the song the old women sings
In this place every morning
Life goes on and time leaves
It leaves by night
The night hides it all
Anything larger than time will be blanked
by the fog that slides down and away from these cliffs
dreams fly away to distant lands here
But the hopes and wants of the lonely hearts will stay
sunrise is the reminder of upcoming Storms
Storms that may take away more than dreams
A strong and sad reality that will inconvenience God
Only because there is no one here to turn to
Those long summer days of pensive time at the garden
Capricious elected tasks that bring your mind to rest
And the old women sing here every morning
They sing for you and for me
Calm waters will be nice for the journey

Shadows and Monsters

Lying down to sleep happy as can be
Grandpa covers me up and gives me a kiss
Saying good night, see you in the morning kid.
He walks out of the room
And I begin to see shadows and monsters
I pull the cover up to my nose—no farther, I need to see
I cough and Grandpa yells
Are you ok buddy?
I respond loud—I am ok!
Shadows and monsters leave
They are afraid of Grandpa
He destroys them just with a look as he points to them
I show him where they hide all the time
He says that I will also destroy them someday soon

But for now he will do it for me
My eyes get heavy I fall asleep and in the morning
No more darkness, happy as can be.

Alvaro Vega

The Professor

The provincial professor showed up with his horses today
The mustang was maimed and destroyed at arrival
all the others were brave
Tomorrow he will pay for
the unseemly scene at Teresa the Austrian's widow
Today he prays and brings here the Padre from San Ignacio's
the one that talks directly with God.
Our Virgin Mary heard it all and he peacefully got lost
He got lost in a world of Christ and Saints where he will dance,
drink and always, always pray.

The Rains

The rains have arrived and the days will get longer.
I will walk in it, because I am without choice
Sadness will also come.
Last season was so hard
I barely made it through the fog
But the clouds cleared and the sun came up in the horizon
I felt alive again.

Spartacus

Spartacus lo vi un verano en película en un garaje cubano
Peleaba con fuerza de héroe un gran ser humano
Abecés sus derrotas me dejaban triste
Al igual que las derrotas de Ulysses
Que ocurrieron en blanco y negro en mi ayer
Dos soldados que quemaron sus historias y legendas
En libros lejanos
Y yo los vi en películas un verano en un garaje cubano

Spartacus

I saw him one summer on film
on the wall of a Cuban garage
He was fighting with the strength of a true hero,
and the shield of a great human being
Sometimes when he was defeated I would be sad
When I think of Ulysses and his defeats
I see two great soldiers
It all happens in black and white in my yesterday

Two soldiers that blazed a place in history
and legends in books far away
And I saw them in film out of an old projector
on the wall of a Cuban garage

Alvaro Vega

Sus Alas Secaran

En el día oscuro de neblina y sol oculto
con árboles y yerba mojada.
Canta un pájaro en la distancia seguro del
mañana.
El sabe que el Sol saldrá que calor le dará
que encontrara su pareja y sus alas secaran
Y por eso canta y por eso está feliz
con su canto trata de comentar
la Buena fortuna que el viento trae
Pocos lo entienden, por eso no lo
desvían de su lindo optimista canto.

The Wings Will Dry

A dark day with fog and the Sun hides
With a wet forest and tall grass
A bird sings in the distance, sure of tomorrow
He knows the Sun will come out and it will get warm again
That he will find his partner, that his wings will dry

And that's why he sings, that's why he is happy
With his song he tries to comment
About the good fortune the wind will bring
Very few understand his song but it doesn't derail him
From his optimistic sonata

The Green Chair

Flick me off the sky so I can see the clouds
my face cold and my heart acid sad
Do your deed, do as you please
Do it
Wrapped in hate or love
It matters not to me
Maybe the others will stare
make the avalanche of slate fall over the ledge
To crash into my pond
Not so much home now
See me
Sitting in the green chair staring at the south blue gray sky
I wait; not sure for what or why
Not yet engaged in reality
Living inside my daydreams
Creeping around in the minds of the unsuspecting
Pulling away photographs that they have discarded
And I collect because I can't stop

Seeing myself inside as a stiff doll with no life
Cat-eyed without depth or reach as my colors change
Scenes of fall and winter days come and go with only
One single spring the day I awaken.

Alvaro Vega

The Water Droplets

Unwillingly resemble Orion
As they fall on the surface of my heart
Today every star completely disappeared
Across the entire universe
So I can see your face
I hope it isn't too cold there
Or lonely
Perhaps I shouldn't bring you so far out there
So often
To satisfy my selfish needs
I don't ask
I never do
I am sorry
If you weren't Earthbound
You would clearly see why

Tell Me How to Pray

I will drop to my knees respectfully
I will remember every word
Also the order in which I must say them
I will show reverence
My eyes will be slightly squinted in case God appears
I think he would be pleased if I don't look at him straight away
I will pray for nine days
all the prayers you have taught me
You will be happy and proud to know
That I will do all this without want
I have nothing to ask for
I have everything I need
I will not ask for favors
Knowing that a wall of humans cry for salvation
I will turn away
From sin

Alvaro Vega

The Broken Mind

She has a broken mind
She knows it in her heart
The little things that make her smile
She keeps
The tiny metal airplane missing a wing
A plastic horse
A gyroscope painted blue
A compass that points to twenty-five degrees northeast always
The music behind her eyes call her to dance naked in the fields
Her body a vessel to the stars
Her mind is glass and bumper cars
Her life is today and never tomorrow
She loves you because you are

you live
If you were gone she wouldn't like it
If you returned she would sing for you
Her mind beautiful and broken.

The Bucket

She grows a small tree inside an old broken bucket
She keeps it on the roof of that old building
Careful not to knock into the temporarily placed posts
that keep her ceiling in place
The posts have lately taken on an old weathered look
No one is coming to fix this mess, this poor excuse of shelter
She wears her favorite blouse and the Canadian necklace
Her earrings she got in Santo Pare
She holds one in her fingers and remembers the evening
Those days were "*fasil*"—easy like Sunday mornings in April
He is gone now a long time and it has rained plenty since
So much so that the lake has gone over twice
Everyone is leaving for higher ground
She holds every single memory
here inside her chest, an appointed task
Sometimes it gets so heavy that it feels
that it soon will explode
Other days not feeling anything,
remembering nothing with empty gaze
Then summer appears and the blinding Sun
The heart begins to work against her, *"no es fasil"*
Exposing treasures that should be guarded once again

Alvaro Vega

The Devil

The devil goes on his walk and everyone
stands still as if frozen
He doesn't see me
He smells everyone like dogs do
I am stealth I wear a cape blessed by God
I am inquisitive in my approach
He smells like death, my skin gets cold
His fangs are bloody, his claws
still have the flesh of lost souls
I am not afraid, am inquisitive
I circle him
He smells me and knows I am there but can't find me
He is enraged and I kick at him
Tempting faith
Am I fooling him completely?
His pulsating cranium thinks
He is a cunning devil; he has a plot afoot
Silly devil
I have a cape blessed by God
If I wanted to return the cape of free will
To be vanquished by this monster
I would not be afraid
I would have lived a great life
and would forever be chained.

To Want With Necessity

Way out here I can hear the sound of your galaxy,
I came out here today because I am so sad,
my heart in great pain
when I am close to you, you're mine completely
when I kiss you, you tell me that you are
then we walk away for this or that
I reach and reach for hope
Hope that someday we stay
When I find a yes I get calm
From here your galaxy is as beautiful as your eyes
From here your galaxy is so alive with everything I love
I feel forces around me, I am never sure if it is Angels or Demons
I reach and I touch your heart
Then you cry for love that you want now,
you want it with necessity, same as I do
It leaves you empty and sad sometimes, I know
I now hold your soul, and your warm body is absent
I come this far so no one sees me crying
To look into your universe that reminds me
With every star the glorious life that is you
My love

About the Author

Alvaro Vega was born in Havana (Habana), Cuba. He was "mostly raised," he explains, by his grandmother because his father was in one of Castro's work camps "granjas" and his mother had to work to feed the family. He was allowed to leave Cuba for the United States in 1973. He now lives in New York.

"In Cuba, I went to Mass often with my grandmother, but it was always a struggle. Going to church was not approved by the government. That made for a greater closeness to church and to the family, I think. But there was also a military aspect to life in Cuba. The military dominated everything, and was part of our way of life.

"My poetry springs from both of these traditions. Writing can be painful, but it also feels good, feels like healing, when it is completed. When I begin, I don't always know where my poetry will end. I want it to be unpredictable."

Index

Alvaro Vega

www.ingramcontent.com/pod-product-compliance
Lightning Source LLC
Chambersburg PA
CBHW031558040426
42452CB00006B/337